# Just My Thoughts

# Don't Judge Me

# Understand My Struggle

By Kemayne Shabazz Smith

ISBN 978-1-62806-157-4

Library of Congress Control Number
2018933367

All Scriptures are taken from the New King
James Version, (Bible Gateway Online)
Copyright, 1982

To contact the author, please feel free to reach
him via email: disdaboyfresh@yahoo.com
or on Facebook at Kemayne Smith.

# *Dedication*

This Book is dedicated to my mother, father, brother, mom-mom, and sons. These individuals mean the world to me; and have inspired me to write this book. While living in my valley, or wilderness experience, I had the opportunity to really build a relationship with God. *And you shall love the Lord your God with all your heart, with all your soul, with all your mind, and with all your strength.' This is the first commandment* (Mark 12:30).

I would like to first "Thank GOD," for allowing me the opportunity to serve Him, through writing this book of poetry, short stories, and my personal thoughts while going through the darkest times of my life. I pray this book will give you courage, insight, and strength while reading about my journey through what I would consider Hell on Earth.

Please know that it was only through the grace and mercy of God that I am still here. He protected me **before**, **during**, **and after** all this has happened to me. I give Him all glory, honor, and praise. *And whatever you do in word or deed, do all in the name of the Lord Jesus, giving thanks to God the Father through Him* (Colossians 3:17). I can personally say it was God who guided and directed my thoughts and pen to write these poems, short stories, and thoughts.

I'd like to acknowledge my mother, Minister Gertrude Cooper. You are a great inspiration and motivation to take my talents, to use my vision, and be a "testimony" for others that may be going through the same struggle. This would never be possible without you - thank you! On March 19, 2017, I was baptized. Mom, I did it - I feel like a new man with a new plan. Old things have died; great things have arrived. I am ready to follow Jesus. To my brother, Trumayne Smith: you give me a reason to live, to strive through these trials and tribulations of every day situations. My children, "We gonna be alright!" Grandma. To my father, Gregory Briddell, thank you for always being there. To my family and loved ones and all the folks that were encouraging me and kept it 100% with me when I was down and going through it - much love! To my Lord and Savior, Jesus Christ, without you, I am nothing! Father, thank you!

This is dedicated to anybody going through something...someone that feels like they can't talk to anyone because they just won't understand...someone out there who just feels different...this is for you. I want you to know God understands and that is all that matters.

# Acknowledgements

Kemayne, through it all, from birth to the present, I have always told you that you are a king of God. I always called you King Kemayne. I am so thankful to God that He had to take you to a place where He could get your full attention, and you could discover, for yourself, who you are. Now, you can see for yourself what I have been telling you all this time; you are a great man of God.

Since God has given you the wisdom to write this book, my prayer for you is this: *The thief does not come except to steal, and to kill, and to destroy. I have come that they may have life, and that they may have it more abundantly* (John 10:10). Me, as your mother, I pray that you have life more abundantly. *I pray that you may prosper in all things and be in good health, just as your soul prospers* (3 John 2).

I love you, and don't let nothing, or nobody stray you away from God. Keep Him first, and mediate on Him in everything you do. I feel that you can conquer anything that life puts before you. God Bless You!

*Your Mother*
*Minister Gertrude (True)*
*Mom!*

# *Just-A-Lil-Talk (With Jesus)*

Woke up this morning (Blessing #1); earlier than usual because of screaming neighbors, bumping and banging on the walls. Mad because I had to work in a few hours. I laid there on the wrong-side of the bed.

Automatically, I started my morning ritual, read my *Daily Bread*, and my Bible Scriptures. Then, because the devil was already trying to start my day off, I decided to pray.

> *Father, I come to you this morning, in the name of Your Son and my Lord and Savior Jesus Christ. Giving You all the honor, all the praise, and all the glory. Thanking You for Your blessings, Your benefits, and Your Word. Lord, I pray You continue to bless my family, my friends, and me. Continue to give us knowledge, wisdom, and understanding. Bless our minds, bodies, and souls, over our hearts, and our health. Provide our every need Lord, in Jesus' name. And Lord strengthen our weaknesses;*

*mentally, physically, emotionally, and spiritually. Now, Lord I have no worries or cares in the world today because I give them to You. Take them Lord and replace them with Your Word, Lord God, that I may be stress-free, in the name of Jesus, Amen.*

The rest of the day was awesome - such a lovely day. Just a little talk with Jesus can brighten your day.

# *A Lost Soul*

Hey brother, can you help me? I can't seem to find my way. I don't even know where it is that I'm trying to get to. I have no friends, my family is not my family, and well...I have nothing.

I have no money and nowhere to stay. All I know is the streets and how to survive. I'm tired of living this way. Having to hurt people, break laws, and do illegal things, by any means, just to eat. Brother, can you help me?

They say there's a place I can get to that will wash away my sins and forgive me. This is a place where I can have family and friends. I don't have to be rich and do evil things anymore. I can have everlasting (eternal) life. All I have to do is believe something. Have you heard of this place? Brother, can you help me?

Listen, I really want to turn my life around and I don't know what to do. I have never asked anybody for help before, but when I saw you today...something touched me and said to me: "This is your brother; he can help you." I'm asking you, "Please! Help me."

## My Wife

She smiles and the sun shines
Beautiful as a flower;
or, as a caterpillar turned butterfly
Her eyes speaking words of love,
inviting me to her lips with a kiss
When she's sad, it's like a rainy day;
cloudy and miserable
Tension, along with the silent-treatment
As we lay; side-by-side our hearts connect
Forced into a moment of passion,
emotions and feelings
Energy is created as chemistry breeds intimacy
Blessed with another day from above,
we manage to stay together
For better or worse, for rich or for poor;
till death come between us
She is more than words; Unexplainable
She is my joy, my pain, my night and my day
She is my inspiration and motivation
My completion and fills the emptiness in my life
And, she is you, My Wife.

# Concrete Jungle

In a world of darkness; evil lurks. Men of all
types; Killers, Drug-Dealers, Rapists, and such
Old Men, Young Men…Convicts and Criminals
Some on a mission for better ways and better
days; a change from old things to new things
and…a different life
While others are confused, and lost; trapped in
a bubble, they struggle to figure it out
Born sinners, we have a choice
that determines the journey
Lock in a Concert Jungle where grown men are
violated and controlled by a system
A system designed to break-a-man-down
He is nothing other than a criminal;
A wild animal
No way out, other than paying dues
Away from things that matter the most
Loved ones, kids, and family
With nothing but time to think…
What will he do?
Will he get stronger and wiser?
Or will he gain anything and lose his soul?
Become institutionalized
Sometimes we get caught up and don't realize
how valuable something is until it's taken away.

# *"Ambition"*

Little Timmy got himself a new bike for his birthday, but this time, his father got him a big-boy bike without the training wheels. This would be a big thing for Timmy, learning how to ride without trainees. So, one Wednesday after work, Timmy's dad had finished mowing the lawn, while his mother was in the flower garden, and he pulled the bike out. Excited and scared at the same time, his mother yelled, "Make sure he has his helmet on, honey." Then, after gearing up, his father says, "Okay, sport, this is your big day. Are you ready?" After little Timmy ran into his mom's car and fell about six good times, he sat on the front step for a while and stared at the bike. With fresh scars and bruises, also without his dad's help this time...Timmy picked his bike up, put the left side pedal up, pushed his bike with a running start, hopped on it and started riding. His father was so amazed to see his boy ride.

See, being a baby in the Word (or in Christ), sometimes (like Timmy), we fall and bruise ourselves, but don't ever give up because the only thing that makes you "a failure" is not trying or giving up. The devil knows your weaknesses, so he expects to win by you giving up; but try harder such as little Timmy did and give "God" the victory. You can be successful.

# *"Trials and Tribulations"*

In June 2013, a young man was arrested for a burglary after a high-speed chase from Maryland to Delaware. Already on the run from other cases pending, when he was caught he had six warrants on top of the new charges. He would spend 10 months in jail waiting for trail. In that time, everyone tells him, "It's going to be alright." His family telling him to pray, and have faith, "God's going to see you through, just believe." His girlfriend/fiancé tells him the same. So now he's praying, talking to God, reading the Word, trying to gain some faith.

Eventually, the young man starts to believe that it's going to be alright and that he would make out.

On March 11, 2014, he was found guilty of first and third degree burglary and convicted. The judge sentence him to 20 years all suspended but 10 and recommended that he do 50% before parole eligibility, with 3 years of probation upon release.

By March 13, 2014 he would be on that bus taking his very first trip to prison. Now, I could just imagine how he must have felt after having faith, praying every day and believing that God would make a way. I could imagine he wanted to ask God why did this happen? How? What did I do wrong? We as believers, and as children of God must first never mix faith with doubt, and never doubt God, because (John 1: 1-3):

- **All things were made through Him, and without Him nothing was made that was made.**

Second, as believers and children of God … another thing we must do is (James 1: 2-7):

- **Count it all joy when you fall into various trails…(v.3), knowing that the testing of your faith produces patience…(v.4), But let patience have it's perfect work, that you may be perfect and complete, lacking nothing…(v.5), If any of you lack wisdom, let him ask of God, who gives to all liberally and without reproach, and it will be given to him… (v.6), But let him ask in faith, with no doubting, for he who doubts is like a wave of the sea driven and tossed by the wind…(v.7), For let not that man suppose that he will receive anything from the Lord.**

We must understand what that means, and in that young man's case, he didn't understand that God has a plan for everybody. Just so happen that God wasn't through with him yet. He felt maybe he needed to sit down for a little while to get his undivided attention, and put the young man back on the right (eons) path. We question God without looking at the full situation, and what He's done.

## Power in Scriptures

Have you ever had problems with Scriptures and trying to understand them? Or have you ever had some Scriptures just stick with you? You know how a Scripture you've read that just does something to you, where you must fellowship with another brother or sister to study it and gain meaning or some knowledge? I have just a few that I like when I hear them. They do something to my soul. It's like something powerful about it.

(Psalms 30:5) *For His anger is but for a moment, His favor is for life; weeping may endure for a night, but joy comes in the morning.* (Wheeewww! That's powerful!)

(Psalms 27: 1) *The Lord is my light and my salvation; whom shall I fear? The Lord is the strength of my life; of whom shall I be afraid?*

(Ephesians 4: 22-24) *And be renewed in the spirit of your mind.*

(Mark 8:36)
*"For what will it profit a man if gains the whole world, and loses his own soul?*

**Some Very Powerful Scriptures!**

# *"Family First"*

I remember when I was a kid, my grandmother used to have this old red and white truck. I mean, an old-school truck, with the gears on the column. And I remember times when grandma would get the whole family together and take us to Strawberry Landing. She'd have us all packed up in the back of that old truck and everything we needed - along with blankets, coolers... All the grandkids and kids would be in the back of the truck (about 10 of us), friends of the family, and the rest of the adults would trial grandma to the spot. When we arrived, we'd all pile-out of the trucks and cars. Some people and kids would get in the water and swim, others would set-up lines and crab. Everyone enjoyed themselves, including grandma. Those were good times. Good family times. I say that to say this: I'm sure everyone remembers when the elders used to keep the family all together? Now, they've passed and it's like "family isn't family no more." Let it not just be a holiday, reunion, or a tragedy, for family to get together. With so many things going on in the world, sickness, and diseases...we might look up one day and realize we never got a chance to say "I love you" or "I'm sorry" or "Goodbye." Or just see them and embrace them before it's too late.

# A Walk In The Park

A beautiful day, sun shining, birds chirping,
the wind slightly blowing,
and the smell of fresh cut grass
Kids on the playground,
laughing and happy
Swing, sliding boards,
money-bars and see-saws
The joy of colors, red, blue, orange, green,
yellow, purple, brown, black, gray, and white
Joggers jogging, skaters skating,
roller-blading, exercising
People reading a novel or magazine,
maybe a newspaper
Just a perfect place to relax
A family of geese strolls by
and heads for the river
Lovers on a blanket having a picnic,
sharing each other's love
As me and Blue (the dog) take a walk
in the park
Nothing major, not too much,
free of charge, not too far from home
Me and my best friend
Walking in the park

# *Love and Hate*

They say it's a thin line between love and hate. How can you love something and so close to hate it? It's such a good feeling to love. Love is God, Happy, Joy, and more. Love is Life. God's greatest gift is Love. Love is a multitude of things. What exactly is Love?

Hate is on the other hand is just the opposite. Not such a good feeling to Hate. Hating something is Anger, Mad, Pain, and more. Hate is Evil. Thou shall not hate. To not like something, to wish bad things, to envy, carry a grudge, have no remorse for something, then you hate it. What exactly is Hate?

Why is there a thin line between love and hate? The two obviously being totally different feelings, and different emotions. They don't mix, but seem to be so easy to transition from one to another. ...When you Hate something, it's hard to ever Love it again. It will never work even if you try, unless you give it to God. As far as Love...

REAL LOVE NEVER DIES! IT WILL ALWAYS BE A LOVE!

# *"Love Lost"*

Have you ever loved someone so much that nothing else really mattered? So much that all you did was try to find new ways to make that someone happy, and let them know that you love them. Going out of your way for gifts, taking them out, trying to impress them, laughing, talking, and spending time together. That's all you want to do is be with that special someone. In the mist of all the love and the relationship, and of course no relationship is 100% perfect, the drama begins. There are arguments, break-ups-to-make-up, fights, and all the things that come with a relationship. Somehow you manage to work through it to stay together because of "Love." Then you think this is the one for you. There's even talk of getting married. A few years pass and things are not perfect, but just okay. Some days are better than others, and some days are dramatic. Anyway, one day, that person who is oh-so-special decides they don't want to be together anymore and they can't do this. Now, after all this time of being in love with this person, everything that you have put into loving them is in the toilet. Heartbroken and torn apart: what do you do?

# *"Things Change"*

"Hey Fresh," the old friend said. "How's it going, brother?"

"How are you feeling?" Fresh said, "Man where have you been, and why are you talking like that?"

"You sound really different, what's up with you?"

"I've been chilling, trying to get my life together, you know," says Fresh. "People change and things change, brother."

"Especially when you're doing the things you used to do. Do you know what I'm saying?" the old buddy says.

"I don't know about all that, but it's good to see you, man. It's been a long time."

"Let's go get some girls, some smokes, and a few gars, homeboy."

Fresh looks at his old buddy and smiles before saying, "You know what, that sounds real nice, but I put all that behind me, man. It used to be fun, I am not going to lie, but man, listen: (1 Corinthian 13: 11) says, 'When I was a child, I spoke as a child, I understood as a child; but when I became a man, I put away childish things.'"

The old friend laughed and said, "That's deep, man. I don't know what happened to the old

Fresh, but the new Fresh is weird."

Fresh said, "That's okay, you'll get there one day. I've got to be though, man; I'm going to pray for you."

The friend just walked away looking confused. Then, all of a sudden, Fresh said, "Hey Dee."

And the friend said, "Yeah man?"

"GOD IS GOOD BROTHER, and prayer changes things."

# *"One of Those Days"* *(Lonely and Depressed)*

*Hebrews 13:5-8*—Lonely
*Psalm 40:1-2*—Depressed

Not feeling like being bothered today. Don't want any company, no phone calls, and not going anywhere. I don't know why I'm in my shell today, but I am, and that's where I'm going to be. Miserable, lonely, and depressed: I'm doing a lot of thinking about this-and-that...thinking about life and the way of the world. I'm just going to just sit here on the couch and eat ice cream, eat cookies, and drown myself in my own misery. Don't need anybody or want anybody else to be miserable with me. Just leave me alone. That's where I'm at today. I was supposed to go to lunch with a friend, but told them, "Maybe another time, not today." They were mad at me, but oh well. I don't feel like it today.

*(Getting to the Scripture)*: Just a couple of things to remember when you get depressed is – [Hebrews 13]

*(Verse #5)* For He Himself has said, "I will never leave you nor forsake you."

*(Verse #8)* Jesus Christ is the same yesterday, today, and forever.

### Psalm 40:1-2

And when you feel depressed remember this –[Psalm 40]

*(Verse #1)* I waited patiently for the Lord; And He inclined to me, and heard my cry.

(Verse #2) He also brought me up out of a horrible pit, out of the miry clay, and set my feet upon a rock, and established my steps.

# *"Count Your Blessing!"*

"What is man, that you are mindful of Him?" For one, let us not ever forget that. In the beginning, God created the heavens and the earth and all things in it. Then let us not ever forget that.

"For God so loved the world that He gave His only begotten Son, that whoever believes in Him should not perish, but have everlasting life."

"For God did not send His Son into the world to condemn the world. He came that the world through Him people might be saved." Then, people, remind yourselves that you have benefits in Jesus.

He forgives.

He heals.

He heals all your diseases.

He redeems your life from destruction.

He crowns you with loving kindness and tender mercies.

He satisfies your mouth with good things so that your youth is renewed like an eagle.

He executes righteousness and judgment for you against oppression. He sets you free.

He makes known His ways to you.

He gives you His grace and mercy in times of need.

I'm mindful of man for everything that he has done for me, and all His benefits, and all His blessings.

God's love is awesome.

# "Momma Said!"

There's always going to be times when things aren't going to go your way.

There's times when it seems like everything and everyone in this world is against you.

Things are going to happen that are going to hurt. "Yes!"

"Go ahead, son, it is okay to cry."

But man-up, stand-firm and move on.

Take the bitter with the sweet.

Everybody falls down. It's a choice you have to make.

"Are you going to stay down?" or "Are you going to get back up?"

There will be times that you will make mistakes. "Nobody is perfect."

"We are all human...born sinners."

"But that doesn't mean that you just accept the mistake."

Master the mistake; take everything you can from that mistake, and "learn from it."

If you don't gain knowledge from making mistakes, then it's likely that they'll be made again.

It's a cold world out here. The world doesn't love you.

You got to get your education, work hard,

handle your priorities and take care of yourself.

And a man is supposed to "provide for his family." (The Head)

Momma said, "I know you better than you know yourself. I'm only telling you these things because I love you. And nobody is going to tell you like Momma."

One day you'll look at your own kids and tell them the same thing. Then you will remember that, that's exactly what Momma said.

# "A Good Friend"

I was speaking to a lady friend of mine that I hadn't seen or spoken to in a very long time. It was someone I grew up with and went to school with. She is a very good friend. And she was telling me about how her man was treating her and threatening to leave her and her kids. As she is crying and confiding in me, I find myself in a situation. Now, I want to be a good friend and give her the best advice, but I'm a man myself, so I don't want to sound like a "hater." So what do I do? Should I let her drown in her own sorrow or should I tell her like it is and the way she needs to hear it from a friend?

Well, me being who I am, I listened to her misery first, and while I was listening to her, I kind of drowned her out and started praying. "Lord, help this woman in her situation to make the right decision for her and her babies. And Lord, bless me with the right friendly advice to give her. Lord give us both strength to carry on, in the name of Jesus, Amen."

After she finished, I said, "You know what, you got to do what's best for you and your kids. You have two beautiful daughters that need you to be strong for them. They don't want see mommy being treated bad by some man. You have them looking up to you for guidance and you don't want them growing up thinking it's cool to just let guys walk all over them. Second of all, you're a good woman. I have known you for a long time. You handle your business, pay your bills, work hard, keep yourself looking good, and your faith to your man. I know you love him, but you don't need anybody who makes you unhappy, disrespects you, your kids, and treats you bad. You deserve so much better, and you can have better. I'm a man myself, and it's not too much we can ask for from a woman who does what you do. Because you love somebody doesn't mean you're obligated to be in an unhappy situation, not satisfied. You can love from a distance. I'm not saying break-up, but if it's not going to work, then you got to figure out what matters most. Do you want happiness for you and your kids or do want to live a lie? It's a choice you have to pray about and make for yourself."

So, I gave it to her straight like that, and she actually listened and thanked me. She said I was right. A week later she called me and said she moved out and is starting her life over with her daughters, and that she was happy about the choice she made.

# *"Un-Known"*

People!

Are you truly grateful and appreciative of God's goodness to us? All of the gifts he gives us. His mercy, His grace and every blessing we receive from Him. Do we take enough time to say, "Thank you, Jesus!" He wakes us up every morning, "Thank you," Father for another day, let us rejoice and be glad. Do we bless our food with grace, and say, "Father, Thank you" for this meal I'm about to receive." May it be blessed and nourish my body. He gives comfort and protection, and to sleep. He gives us clothes to wear, and shelter for sleep. Do we thank Him for these things? See, God is good all the time, and all the time God is good. He loves us and is always blessing us. It is only right to give Him the honor, praise, and glory that He so deserves with a simple, "Lord, I thank you." "Thank you, Jesus." "Hallelujah!" Folk, be 100% grateful every time God blesses you, because even though He will always be there and never forsake you, He don't have to. He still does what He says He says He will do. Think about it when you didn't have the things you have and remember how you got them. Little things, big things, all things: God made it happen.

# *"I Need An Answer: Lord, Speak To Me!"*

I was thinking about my girlfriend, and the conversation we had a few nights ago, about us getting right with God, and renewing our lives together. It's funny how when I opened my Bible, I went right to 1 Corinthians, chapter 7. Man, as I started, it became clear to me. "This is deep," I said to myself, "either God is speaking to me, or the Spirit brought me to this Scripture." It starts by talking about because of sexual immorality, each man should have his own wife and each woman her own husband. Then it talked about how they should render the affection due each other. The wife does not have authority over her body, the husband does; and likewise, the wife over the husband. Do not despise one another; you may come together in fasting and praying, so that Satan does not tempt your lack of self-control. Now, Chapter 8; this is where I felt something; because my girlfriend and I have been speaking about marriage. Verse #8 says, but I say to the unmarried and the widow: It is good for you to remain even as I am. Verse #9 says, but if they cannot exercise self-control, let them marry. For it is better to marry than to burn with passion. I just think it is amazing how I and my lady were just having a conversation about getting married - no longer living in sin - and renewing our lives together with Christ. I, myself, prayed about it and asked the Lord for guidance, and reveal to me the right direction to go with this. Over the years I've learned that sometimes in the decision-making process, some things you have to pray about, and ask God for that help in making the right decision. For me, it's everything that I go to Him for answers. I've made too many bad choices in my life, so I use a Higher Power; and He's been there every time. Now tonight I was thinking about that conversation, and when I picked up my Bible, He gave me this Word. "He is Awesome! Well, I guess I'm getting married!

# *"Keep Blessing!"*

"Hey Tom!"

"Good morning, Bill, how you feeling?"

"Oh, alright, I guess. What's up?"

"What do you mean, you guess?"

"Well, you know I've been sick. I got arthritis in my hand and feet, and my back is killing me. Went to the doctors yesterday and he gave me these pills to take; and the on top of that... He tells me I may have to lose my legs. He says I'll never walk again."

"Hey, listen to me Bill, you have to start taking care of yourself man. I see you out here every day, waiting on the liquor store to open; then you're drunk all day."

"Yeah Tom, that's easy for you to say; look at you, you have a good job, wife, kids, a nice home, and living good. Me...I have nothing."

"You don't have to live like you're living, man; you choose that life. Me, I'm blessed, nobody gave me this house these cars, and my wife. I worked hard and got myself up off this corner and started going to Church. If anything, God blessed me with what I have."

"Ah man, the Church don't want to see no old-fart like me. They'll just look at me and laugh.

"Bill, the only people laughing are them doctors, and people behind that cash register, you keep giving your money to, buying that alcohol. Do not worry about what people say, they are always going to talk about you, especially when you're doing right. These doctors can't do what God can do for you, brother. Listen, I have a good buddy of mine; and his father was bad-off; real sick. The doctors gave him a certain amount of time to live. They told him he would not make it. "Guess what?"

"What?"

"He's still living today, by the grace of God. I'm telling you, Bill, clean yourself up and start believing in God. Doors will open for you; I guarantee you, your life will turn around. Try it and if it does not work for you, I'll never bother you again. You have to start somewhere. What do you say? I'll see you Sunday, right?"

"Yeah, I guess so!"

"Good, don't let me down; and just come as you are, and you'll be fine."

*Two or Three Months Later...*

"Hey Tom! Church service was good last Sunday man. I'm on my way to work. I'll see you tonight at Bible study."

"Okay, Bill. Hey, remember that morning, on

the corner, when told you how your life would turn around? Boy, look at you! You have a good job, pickup truck, looking good, and everything."

"Yes, I remember, brother; and thanks. I'm alcohol, and drug-free; clean for three months, taking no pills, and I'm feeling great. I appreciate that inspiration; for real."

"Hey, no problem. Anything I can help a brother and save a soul; just keep believing."

*Proverbs 12:4* — *An excellent wife is the crown of her husband, but she who causes shame is like rottenness in his bones.*

"Wow!"

What does that mean? What is God saying? It caught my attention, and I'd just like to elaborate on that. Just recently I was having a chat with a buddy, and he was telling me how happy he was that his girlfriend (even though he referred to her as his wife), was "keeping it real" while he was in prison, and that the baby-girl that she had five months ago that they had made while he was at pre-release, before he violated the rules and got sent back to population, was getting big. He said she was answering phone calls, putting money on his books, and being faithful. He was talking about marrying her. I could see it in his face that he was really excited, and I didn't want to "shoot him off of his horse," so I just asked him, "Are you sure?" Anyway, the following week he comes to me looking "emotionally sick," talking about the baby's not his, and he found out a bunch of other disloyal things about her. So, getting back to the Scripture, on how it relates (from my point of view) is this: when he saw her as (excellent), "keeping it real," she was the best thing in his life; she made him happy and content. She was his crown. But as soon as he realized that all of that was a front, she was cheating and doing other things; **it broke his heart, hurt his pride, caused him shame like rottenness in his bones.** See, when a man meets a woman or a boy meets a girl; there's an automatic energy that flows. If they like each other, they date and hook-up and establish a relationship. Believe it or not, women play a major role in men's lives as well as a man in a woman's life. It's no different than Adam and Eve: (Mark 10:6-9); *"But, from the beginning of the creation, God make them male and female"* (V.7). *For this reason a man shall leave his father and mother and be joined to his wife,* (V.8). *And the two shall become one flesh; so then they are no longer two, but one flesh* (V.9). *"Therefore, what God has joined together, let no man separate."* Meaning that once you make a commitment, it's really not lawful to break-up or divorce. Moses permitted a man (or woman) to write a certificate of divorce and to dismiss her (him). Most of the time, people fall in love and get married because it's the thing to do, but as soon as it doesn't work out, they divorce (V.9). *"Let not man separate."* At least try to fight for it, to make it work and save the marriage first, unless it wasn't really True Love to begin with. The Bible says … LOVE NEVER FAILS!"

# *"Addiction"*

Wednesday night, I was watching a show that came on the National Geographic television channel called "Drug, Inc." I was watching how there are so many people in this country that are addicted to drugs or something illegal. Some people are addicted to selling drugs or guns. Some buy guns to rob and some to steal. Not only did it make me realize how bad it is in the world with the drug industry, it also made me remember my experiences with drugs, the hustle, and the addiction. But, I came a long way from that point of my life and found a better addiction, which brought me to this thought while I was watching: if we put the time and effort that we put into our addictions into God, what kind of change would happen in the world? And I say this because I turned my life around from what I used to be, but I remember how much time, money, thought, and effort went into it. Now, I give all of that to the Lord. It's not just drugs either. People have shopping addictions, sex, money, cars, and all sorts of worldly desires. These are addictions also. My Bible says, "*Let no one say when he is tempted, I am tempted by God; for God cannot be tempted, by evil, nor does He Himself tempt anyone.*" But each one is tempted by his own desires and enticed.

Then when desire has conceived, it gives birth to sin; and sin, when it is full-grown, brings forth death. For some people, their additions may be hard to just give up and surrender. Some may say it's just a thing that's all in one's head, but nothing on this planet is too hard for God. It can be defeated. A lot of the problem is that the devil has people trapped in his world and they think it's no other way (Proverbs 14:12). There is a way that seems right to a man, but it's end is the way of death. (James 4:7): *"Therefore, submit to God, Resist the devil, and he will flee from you."*

# *"My Testimony"*

I'm sitting in service, every Sunday, and every Sunday, the speaker asks, "Does anyone have a testimony they would like to share?" And, I am ready to go up and share, but my thoughts aren't together, and I get a bit nervous. Then, as I listen to some of the other brothers give theirs, I'm thinking, "Mine is very similar to everybody else's. I can relate to a lot of those brothers." Then I start feeling like because I wanted to go up and didn't, then I let God down. He called me once again and I didn't answer.

See, God has called me various times, and I didn't hear Him; plus, my mother is a minister, and her husband is an elder as well. So I get it from every angle, telling me, "You're a king. You should be preaching God's Word." But I never look at myself as a preacher. But I was sitting in my room thinking about my testimony, because it has really been getting to me. Now, from my understanding, and mind you, I'm still seeking knowledge and wisdom of the Word, but a testimony is supposed to be your story of how you found God, or received Him. Your testimony is your story of what God has done for you in your life. That's how it was explained to me. So I looked up the definition of the word "testimony" in *Webster's Dictionary* and it says, "a statement testifying to benefits received." After looking up the meaning, I am now ready to share my story at this Sunday's service. I don't know exactly why I was so nervous and intimidated about giving my testimony, but God said, "Watch, stand-fast in the faith, be brave, be strong."

Sometimes we let fear and thoughts of someone else's judgment take us off course from what we were called to do. But, we have to pray and keep our focus on one thing… and that is The Lord.

"Nothing else matters!"

# *"Sometimes"*

Sometimes I'm happy. I just want to laugh and enjoy the moment.

Sometimes I just want to relax and be at peace. Read a book (perhaps the Bible).

There are times when I feel alone, and love to have the company of family and friends.

Then sometimes, I just want to be by myself; in my shell - me, myself, and I.

Sometimes I get emotional, I just want to cry. It seems like there's no end to the sadness, the drama, the stress, depression, etc.

Sometimes I fall on my face and pray. Prayer keeps me sane, humble; prayer strengthens me. It helps me in a lot of ways.

Sometimes I just want to talk, confide in someone, express my feelings, and let it all out. Then, sometimes, I just listen. Take a walk, look at life, God's creation and listen to the animals.

Sometimes I just sit in silence and think.

So, many thoughts come to mind. It is amazing. I then close my eyes and visualize, let my mind just wander. I have many visions. I walk to the beat of my own drum, in my own little world, and sometimes I examine myself. I am who I am, I can be me. If you don't love yourself, how can someone else love you? I love myself. Don't judge me.

# *"Everyday Praise"*

*Psalms 41: 7-10*

- (v. 7): All who hate me whisper together against me; against me they devise my hurt.
- (v. 8): An evil devise say, "cling to him. And now that he lies down, he will rise up no more."
- (v. 9): Even my own familiar friend in whom I trusted, who ate my bread, has lifted up his heel against me.
- (v. 10): But you, O Lord, be merciful to me, and Rise me up, that I may repay them.

I used to walk around with this burden on my shoulder about everyone that has done me wrong in any kind of way. I went in my shell and cut a lot of folks out of my life. Everyone was a suspect to me. I just had a lot of anger running through my veins and I hated people and wanted them hurt or to hurt them. Then I was in a situation with a supposed friend that I trusted like a brother. I invited him into my momma's house, and broke bread with him. Not everybody gets that privilege. So when he did me wrong in our little situation, I felt some type of way, and the very first thing that came to mind was...WAR!!! But, I was disciplined by God with time to think about anger, friends, and forgiveness. As far as friends, I've learned…

*Proverbs 18:24* — A man who has friends must himself be friendly, but there is a friend who sticks closer than a brother. Then, I learned about anger. "Vengeance is Mine, says the Lord."

Forgiveness is *Colossians 3: 13* — Bearing with one another, and forgiving one another. If anyone has a complaint against another, even as Christ forgave you, so you also must do.

Let the peace of God rule in your hearts

# *Knowing*

To wake-up every morning and be able to see your face...is knowing. Knowing that when you kiss me before walking out the door, whether it be for work, or whatever reason, that you will be coming back to me...Knowing that if we are not together, that no matter where you are...without a shadow of a doubt, I can trust you. Knowing that nothing or no one could come between this love and level of understanding we share. Regardless of the situation, the odds against us, the obstacles in the way, along with everything that has tried to destroy us...at the end of the day, it's knowing that you are with me that keeps me sane and gives me strength. I don't have to worry, because I know...

# *"Fix It"*

Let it not be just an occasion, a holiday, or a tragedy for families to come together. Look around at the faces you see; then think about all the faces you don't see. The people who are missing, either gone on up to heaven, or somewhere doing their own thing. With family being so separated, we have to think about what is real and what is important. Family is everything. So much going on in the world today, you can't take life for granted. You never know when you might not ever be able to say "I love you" to your brother, sister, mom, dad, aunt, uncle, niece, nephew, grandma, grandpa, cousin, or whoever... "I love you." You just don't know when it could be too late to say "I'm sorry." And, of course, we never think about it until it's too late. So these holidays and so forth...put your differences aside, and if there is something in between you and a loved-one, FIX IT. Sometimes, it only takes a phone call just to say "Hey, what's up?" or "Are you good?" or get together and do lunch, but at the end of the day, it's all about family. Family First. How can you enjoy someone else's family when your family is messed-up? So let's get it together and make family strong again like when the elders had things under control. It's our generation up next to keep the family strong and together.

# *Untitled*

After going through tough times, and coming from the dark places that I have been in my life, learning and growing from these experiences… it makes me think a lot and observe more. For some reason, I find myself just staring at myself in the mirror, kind of "examining me," and I had a question… "What do folks see when they look at me?" While thinking about that, it also came to my mind of how we judge things just by the outer appearance, whether it be a person, food, place, or whatever. For example, you may have said or heard someone say, "I don't like him/her, they just look like they aren't no good." Or, how kids be like, "Ew, I don't like it," but they never had it or tried it (food), as well as in the first example, you don't know him/her. Now, have you ever wondered why people talk bad about you for no reason? They hate on you and come off on you the wrong way. The whole time you may not let it hinder you, or keep you from moving forward, but let's admit that at least once you have thought in your mind, "Why? I have done no wrong to this person."

Now, without knowing someone, you don't like them. But in reality, you don't even know for sure if you like them or not, because you don't even know them. Before you be quick to judge me, get to know me; sit down and have a conversation with me, and try to understand my story, my struggle, where I came from, what I've been through, and how I overcame; then judge me from that, if you want to, but until then you don't know anything about me except what you see on the outside.

# A Mother's Love

There is a special bond between a mother and her child. A bond that is unbreakable. It is established when she discovers she has a baby in her womb. A love for that baby is formed. A love like none other.

To top that off, the birth of a baby, having to carry for nine months, to go through this massive pain, but the joy of that comes after the pain. When that child is hungry, a mother's love feeds. When that child cries, a mother's love comforts and makes them feel safe. She does all the things that a mother does to raise her child; teach her child and care for her child. Things that are unforgettable and irreplaceable.

Sons will grow up, become men, and go off to seek a soulmate (or someone to love). Daughters will become women to wait for their husband, to love them. But no one can replace that kind of love you get from mom.

I remember my mother used to say, "Ain't nobody gonna love you like momma do." And sometimes it may see like nobody "feels you" or understands you. My mother would say, "I know you better than you know yourself. Mommy knows when something is wrong with you; I can feel it." And until this day, she has made me believe that, because whenever I have something going on, it seems like she knows, and vice versa. It's like I can feel my mother, when it's time to call her or go see her. A mother's love - I wouldn't trade it in for anything.

# "Thanks, Momma!"

For carrying me in your belly for 9-months.

For the labor pains of birthing me, clothing me, and all the hard work to keep a roof over our heads.

For all the nights, I heard you praying and crying. Too young to understand, I never asked you why? But, now I get it. The struggle brings you pain.

For always making a way. Always being there.

For teaching me right from wrong.

For the disciple and punishments when I messed-up.

For always listening and always telling me, "Baby, it's going to be alright."

For old-fashioned values and rules. Household chores. For making us go to Church (Sunday School).

For not just being a mother, but sometimes a Father too. And sometimes a friend as well. Things I couldn't talk to anybody about, you understood, and made me feel comfortable, without judging. Most of all for the love. And as I got older, for the "tough-love" when I was hotheaded and rebellious.

For all the stress, I've caused you...the hurt and the pain...and times I messed-up bad.

For the disappointments.

For never giving up on me. And always being in my corner, whether right or wrong. Mom, I just want to say "Thank you!" Thank you for always being a mother first; and then for being the strong woman that you are. I love to say "Thank you" for so many things, but it'll never be enough. You will always be my favorite girl; my First Lady. Momma, "I love you." Because of you, I am a man today. "Thank you!"

# "How Can You Say That You Love Me?"

How can you say that you love me, when clearly you don't? How can you say that you love me and treat me this way? You said you would always be my friend, and I could always count on you, but when I needed you the most, you turned your back on me. How can you say you love me? Is it just something you think I want to hear, or do you just play with love? Do my feelings matter to you? The pain you've given me and your actions show no signs of remorse or sorrow; yet you continue to tell me you love me.

Maybe you hate me? But why? I'm not perfect; I have flaws, but I stand as I am. I said I would always be here for you; I'd always be a friend, and I keep my word. That hasn't changed, but you have. Do you even know what love is? (1 Corinthians 13: 4-8): *Love is patient, love is kind. It does not envy, it does not boast. It is not proud, it is not rude. It is not self-seeking, it is not easily angered. It keeps no records of wrong. Love does not delight in evil, but rejoices with the truth. It always protects, always trust, hopes; always preservers. Love never fails.*

How can you say you love me? You don't show any kind of affection or compassion. I must wonder, where did I go wrong? Even though it hurts to know that your love is not true...I must let that go and move on. So, I pray for you. I give my feelings to God because he cares for me and...really, all I need is his love. It the only love that matters anymore. You don't have to tell me you love me no more. You and I both know that you don't. Just know that. I'm fine with the truth, but be honest with yourself. You'll feel better about it.

# The Song

The Song says, "I won't go back, I can't go back, to the way it used to be, before Your presence came and saved me." WOW! That automatically makes me think of the goodness of the Lord, and all that He has done for me. All that He has brought me through. And how, though I didn't deserve anything, He chose me. God loved me when I didn't love Him. I was in the world, and the world was in me. I was just a sinner in every way. But, God still was patient with me. He took the time to wait on me. I had hit rock-bottom and had nothing...nobody to turn to. It was God, still there, still working, still waiting, and ready for me to surrender. Once I made the choice, God saved me and still accepted me. So, when I count my blessings, and think of how great He has been, and still is... How could I go back to what He saved me from. Would He have sacrificed His only begotten Son? "No!" I'm free; no longer bound, no more chains holding me. My soul is resting; it's just a blessing...Praise the Lord; Hallelujah, "I'm free!" As the Lord is faithful, and keeps His promises, so should we be. And as we grow in grace, there will always be temptation. Just remember the He will never leave you nor forsake you. And He will always make a way of escape.

# Psalm 57

Have mercy on me, O God, have mercy on me,
for in you my soul takes refuge.
I will take refuge in the shadow of your wings
until the disaster has passed.
I cry out to God Most High,
to God, who fulfills his purpose for me.
He sends from heaven and saves me,
rebuking those who hotly pursue me,
God sends his love and his faithfulness.
I am in the midst of lions;
I lie among ravenous beasts -
men whose teeth are spears and arrows,
whose tongues are sharp swords.
Be exalted, O God, above the heavens;
let your glory be over all the earth.
They spread a net for my feet -
I was bowed down in distress.
they dug a pit in my path -
but they have fallen into it themselves.
My heart is steadfast, O God,
my heart is steadfast,
I will sing and make music.
Awake, my soul!
Awake, harp and lyre!
I will awaken the dawn.
I will praise you, O Lord, among the nations;

I will sing of you among the peoples.
For great is your love, reaching to the heavens;
Your faithfulness reaches to the skies.
Be exalted, O God, above the heavens;
let your glory be over all the earth.

David has a perfect exaple here in this prayer of how we should handle situations in time sof trouble. Times of abuse (physical or verbal) or when the enemy comes at us, rather than stoop to the level of foolishness or give them the satisfacation of worrying, stressing, and acting crazy over the problem ... how to talk to God and let God be our defense. David's example shows how to praise God when we face trials and not to waste time  worrying when  you can invest that time in God who gives us confidence.

# *Somebody's Watching Me*

So, you are a Christian, right? You consider yourself a child of God, a believer, saved and sanctified, holy and righteous. Okay, but what about when no one is watching, or outside of the church, or in the privacy of your home? How do you act amongst non-believers or unsaved souls? How do you respond to negativity, violence, bad situations, verbal or physical abuse? What kind of language are you using when outside church? Who are your friends or who do you associate with? Does church only start on Sunday? Or does church start when you have an issue? Are you holy and righteous when trials come, when storms come, when the chips are down, when your husband or wife gets on your nerves, when the kids are acting crazy? Are you cussing folks out because you had a bad day or because you are in a bad mood? How are you acting, speaking, and living outside of the church, or when no one is there?

Folks, have we forgotten? When we become born-again, when we accept Christ into our lives as believers and children of God, we have this thing called "The Holy Spirit" in us. So, basically, we have Christ in us no matter where we are, what we do — he is in us. Therefore, when you

think no one is around, or that you are alone ....
Just remember that you carry the spirit of the
Lord inside of you. Besides that, God knows all
and sees all. We will be held accountable. We
have to be careful how we live our lives daily.
There is a higher standard for Christians and believers, especially for pastors, ministers, preach-
ers, teachers, and those who deliver the message.
To be in that position, you have to be Christ-like
so there's certain things you absolutely cannot do
and there's a certain way you have to live because
you would not see Christ living any other way
than holy and righteous.

We have to be examples of Christ.

*What has God done for you today?*

*What have you done for God today?*

✝

*I heard the voice of the Lord saying,*
*"Whom shall I send, and who will go for us?"*
*Then I said, "Here I am! Send me."*

**Isaiah 6:8**